THE FIRST TELEPHONE

By Catherine Chambers

Reconstruction of Bell's workshop

First telephone to transmit words

Alexander Graham Bell (centre)

Series Editor Deborah Lock
Project Editor Caryn Jenner
Editor Rohini Deb
Art Editor Yamini Panwar
Senior Art Editor Ann Cannings

Producer, Pre-production Ben Marcus
DTP Designers Syed Md. Farhan, Anita Yadav
Picture Researcher Nishwan Rasool
Managing Editor Soma B. Chowdhury
Managing Art Editor Ahlawat Gunjan
Art Director Martin Wilson

Reading Consultant
Maureen Fernandes

First published in Great Britain by
Dorling Kindersley Limited
80 Strand, London, WC2R 0RL

Copyright © 2015 Dorling Kindersley Limited
A Penguin Random House Company
10 9 8 7 6 5 4 3 2 1
001—271727—Sept/2015

A CIP catalogue record for this book
is available from the British Library

ISBN: 978-0-2411-8283-3

Printed and bound in China.

The publisher would like to thank the following for their kind permission to reproduce their photographs:
(Key: a-above; b-below/bottom; c-centre; f-far; l-left; r-right; t-top)

1 Alamy Images: Pictorial Press Ltd (b). Getty Images: SSPL (cr). Science Photo Library: Carol M. Highsmith Archive, Library of Congress (cl). 3 Dreamstime.com: Konstant Kirillov (tr). 5 Alamy Images: The Print Collector (c). 7 Alamy Images: Niels Poulsen nu. (b). Science Photo Library: Sheila Terry (t). 9 Dreamstime.com: Tunarddda (br). 10 Dreamstime.com: Sergii Kolesnyk (b). 10–11 Dreamstime.com: Konstantin Kirillov (t). 12–13 Dreamstime.com: Konstanti Kirillov (t). 13 Alamy Images: Historic Collection (b). 14 Alamy Images: Everett Collection Historical (br) Corbis: Bell Collection / National Geographic Creative (bl). The Library of Congress, Washington DC: (tr, cl). 15 Corbis: Bell Family / National Geographic Creative (t). The Library of Congress, Washington DC: (cr, b). 16 Dreamstime.com: Fdmsd8yea (c). 19 Science Photo Library: Claus Lunau (c). 20–21 Dreamstime.com: Sergii Kolesnyk. 22 The Library of Congress, Washington DC: (b 23 The Library of Congress, Washington DC: (c). 24 Science Photo Library: Sheila Terry (t). 24–25 Dreamstime.com: Konstantin Kirillov. 25 Alamy Images: North Win Picture Archives (c). 26–27 Dreamstime.com: Konstantin Kirillov. 26 Dorling Kindersley: The Science Museum, London (cr). Dreamstime.com: Wissanustock (clb). Getty Images: Science & Society Picture Library (b). 28–29 Dreamstime.com: Konstantin Kirillov (t). 29 Dreamstime.com: Mcarrel (b). 30 Alamy Images: Classic Image (c) Dorling Kindersley: The Science Museum, London (b). 31 Corbis: GraphicaArtis (t). Dorling Kindersley: The National Cycle Collection (b). 32 The Library of Congress, Washington DC: (cl). 32–33 Dreamstime.com: Andrej Kaprinay. 33 Dreamstime.com: Tamas. 34 Getty Images: Boyer (t). 34–35 Dreamstime.com: Yurikr (tr). 35 The Library Congress, Washington DC: (tr). 36 Science Photo Library: Sheila Terry (t). 36–37 Dreamstime.com: Konstantin Kirillov (t). 37 Science Photo Library: Carol M. Highsmith Archive, Library of Congress (b). 38–39 Dreamstime.com: Konstantin Kirillov (t). 39 Dreamstime.com: Vlntn (br). 40–41 Dreamstime.com: Cekur; Konstantin Kirillov (t). 42–43 Dreamstime.com: Konstantin Kirillov (t). 43 Corbis: Leemage (br). 44 The Library of Congress, Washington DC: (b). 44–45 Dreamstime.com: Konstantin Kirillov (t) 45 Dreamstime.com: Mcarrel (c). 48 Science Photo Library: Sheila Terry (t). 48–49 Dreamstime.com: Konstantin Kirillov (t). 49 Getty Images: Hulton Archive (c). 50 Gett Images: Universal History Archive (c). 50–51 Dreamstime.com: Konstantin Kirillov. 52–53 Dreamstime.com: Konstantin Kirillov (t). 53 Getty Images: Universal History Archive (c). 54–55 Dreamstime.com: Konstantin Kirillov (t). 55 Dreamstime.com: Mcarrel (b). 56–57 Dreamstime.com: Konstantin Kirillov (t). 57 Corbis: (c). 58 Bridgema Images: Museum of the City of New York, USA (c). 58–59 Dreamstime.com: Konstantin Kirillov (t). 60–61 Dorling Kindersley: The Science Museum, London (c). 64 Alamy Images: North Wind Picture Archives (bl); Old Paper Studios (t). The Library of Congress, Washington DC: (tl, tr). 66 Science Photo Library: Sheila Terry (t). 66–67 Dreamstime.com: Konstantin Kirillov (t). 67 Corbis: Anu Dayal / Illustration Works (br). 68 Corbis: (bc). 68–69 Dreamstime.com: Konstantin Kirillov (t). 70–71 Dreamstime.com: Konstantin Kirillov (t). 71 Dreamstime.com: Dynsimages (bc). 72–73 Dreamstime.com: Konstantin Kirillov (t). 73 The Library of Congress, Washington DC: (c). 74 Alamy Images: Everett Collection Historical (bc). 74–75 Dreamstime.com: Konstantin Kirillov (t). 75 Alamy Images: Everett Collection Historical (t). Dreamstime.com: Mcarrel (b). 76–77 Dreamstime.com: Konstantin Kirill (t). 77 The Library of Congress, Washington DC: (b). 78 Corbis: (c). Science Photo Library: Sheila Terry (t). 79 Science Photo Library: Sheila Terry (b). 80 The Library Congress, Washington DC: (cra, bl). 80–81 Dreamstime.com: Daboost. 81 The Library of Congress, Washington DC: (tl, tr, bl). 82 Science Photo Library: Sheila Terry (t 82–83 Dreamstime.com: Konstantin Kirillov (t). 83 Getty Images: SuperStock (t). 84 The Library of Congress, Washington DC: (c). 84–85 Dreamstime.com: Konstantin Kirillov (t). 86–87 Dreamstime.com: Konstantin Kirillov (t). 87 Corbis: Tetra Images (t). 88–89 Dreamstime.com: Konstantin Kirillov (t). 89 Dreamstime.com: Mcarrel (b). 90 TopFoto.co.uk: The Granger Collection (tr). 94–95 Dreamstime.com: Konstantin Kirillov (t). 94 Science Photo Library: Sheila Terry (t). 95 Dreamstime.com: Mcarrel (b). 96–97 Dreamstime.com: Konstantin Kirillov (t). 97 Dreamstime.com: Mcarrel (cb). 98–99 Dreamstime.com: Konstantin Kirillov (t). 99 Getty Images: SSPL (cr). 100–101 Dreamstime.com: Mcarrel (c). 101 Corbis: Gordon Osmundson (cr). 102–103 Dreamstime.com: Konstantin Kirillov (t). 103 The Library of Congress, Washington DC: (cb). 104–105 Dreamstime.com: Konstantin Kirillov (t). 105 Getty Images: Mansell (c). 106–107 Corbis: Stefano Bianchetti. 108 Alamy Images: Everett Collection Historical (b). Corbis: Tarker (t). 108–109 Dreamstime.com: Svetlana Smirnova. 109 Alamy Images: The Print Collector (t). Corbis: Tarker (b). 112 Science Photo Library Sheila Terry (t). 112–113 Dreamstime.com: Konstantin Kirillov (t). 114–115 Dreamstime.com: Konstantin Kirillov (t). 115 The Library of Congress, Washington DC. 116–1 Dreamstime.com: Georgios Kollidas. 118 Dorling Kindersley: The Science Museum, London (cr). 122–123 Dorling Kindersley: The Science Museum, London

Jacket images: Front: Alamy Images: The Print Collector cl; Sunshine Pics cb. Dorling Kindersley: The Science Museum, London clb, bl. Dreamstime.com: Adum88x c; Andreykuzmin cr; Bagwold tc; Galló Gusztáv / Gallofoto tr; Ian Poole / ianpoole br. Back: Science Photo Library: Carol M. Highsmith Archive, Library of Congress.

All other images © Dorling Kindersley
For further information see: www.dkimages.com

A WORLD OF IDEAS:
SEE ALL THERE IS TO KNOW
www.dk.com

CONTENTS

Alexander's Ideas

How do people speak to each other? How do they hear? How can people send and receive messages more easily and more quickly? These questions fascinated Alexander Graham Bell.

His life's work was improving communication, defined as 'the exchange of information, thought or feeling so that it is received or understood'.

Alexander and his father helped deaf people to communicate, teaching them to speak despite not being able to hear. Alexander was also interested in making communication over long distances easier and quicker.

Before Alexander invented the telephone, people sent messages by writing letters that were transported by ship, train or horseback. If they wanted their message to arrive sooner, they sent it by telegraph.

Alexander Graham Bell had a better idea. What if people could actually speak to each other over long distances?

Alexander
Graham
Bell

THE TELEGRAPH

Alexander Graham Bell was inspired to invent the telephone while working on improvements for the electric telegraph.

HOW TO SEND A MESSAGE BY TELEGRAPH

1 Bring your message to a telegraph office.

2 The telegraph operator taps out your message on the telegraph transmitter. Short messages are best!

3 Each letter is sent as an electrical signal to the receiving telegraph office. Telegraph wires on poles link the telegraph offices.

4 A telegrapher converts the electrical signals back into letters to decode the message.

5 The written telegram is then delivered by hand.

CONNECTING CONTINENTS

In 1858, the first transatlantic telegraph cables connected Europe and North America. Telegraph wires connected Australia to Europe in 1872.

MORSE CODE

In 1837, American Samuel Morse devised a code of short and long signals known as 'dots' and 'dashes'. Morse code is still used around the world.

A . _	J . _ _ _	S . . .
B _ . . .	K _ . _	T _
C _ . _ .	L . _ . .	U . . _
D _ . .	M _ _	V . . . _
E .	N _ .	W . _ _
F . . _ .	O _ _ _	X _ . . _
G _ _ .	P . _ _ .	Y _ . _ _
H	Q _ _ . _	Z _ _ . .
I . .	R . _ .	

◄ ## ABC TELEGRAPH

In 1840, British inventor Charles Wheatstone built an ABC telegraph with a needle that paused at the correct letter on the dial.

Wheatstone's
ABC telegraph

SURROUNDED BY SOUND

Alexander listened to his mother playing the piano. When she finished, he clapped enthusiastically. It fascinated him that she played such beautiful music even though she was deaf and couldn't hear it.

Alexander asked his mother if he could look inside the piano. When he spoke to her, he used a low voice and leaned very close to her forehead. Alexander was sure his mother could hear him when he spoke to her in this way.

His mother stood up from the piano stool to give him space. Alexander was a curious boy and was always investigating things. She didn't mind.

Alexander got some tools and took the lid off the piano. He saw that when he pressed a piano key, it caused a hammer to hit a string, which then vibrated. The sound of the piano came from the vibrating strings.

He noticed that the sounds of other musical instruments were made with vibrations too. He also had an idea that his mother could 'hear' the vibrations of his voice when he spoke to her.

Alexander Bell was born on 3rd March, 1847, in Edinburgh, the capital city of Scotland. He added the middle name 'Graham' when he was 11.

Aleck, as he was known, was surrounded by the exploration of sound and voices. His father, Melville Bell, taught elocution, helping people pronounce sounds and words clearly. Mr Bell was particularly interested in teaching deaf people to speak. This was tricky because they couldn't hear sounds to copy them. At the time, deaf people mainly communicated using sign language.

American Sign Language for BELL

Mr Bell felt that the ability to speak would help deaf people participate more fully in a hearing world. Aleck's mother was a good example.

As a teenager, Aleck visited his grandfather in London, where he saw a demonstration of a 'speaking machine'. An air flow, like breathing, was created by bellows, and a vibrating reed made different sounds, and even words.

At home, Mr Bell challenged Aleck and his brother, Melville, Jr, to make their own speaking machine. Their contraption had a windpipe, vocal cords and a mouth with lips. Melville blew through the windpipe, while Aleck moved the lips.

"Ma-ma!" said the machine, and the whole family burst into laughter.

Later, Aleck experimented on the family dog, moving the dog's mouth so that his growls sounded like words.

By age 16, Aleck was teaching elocution like his father. He and his two brothers also helped their father demonstrate Visible Speech. This was the system of written symbols devised by Mr Bell to show deaf people how to make the sounds needed for speech.

Aleck was fascinated by the work of German physicist Hermann Von Helmholtz, who used a variety of devices to make speechlike sounds. Aleck often went to the telegraph office to send messages that were transmitted using signals over an electrical wire. What if people could actually speak to each other over a wire? The idea of transmitting voices stuck firmly in Aleck's head.

Sadly, Aleck's two brothers died of a lung disease called tuberculosis. His parents worried that he would get sick too. They decided to move where the air was cleaner. In July 1870, when Aleck was 23, the family moved across the Atlantic Ocean to Brantford, Ontario, in Canada.

A year later, Aleck moved again. This time to Boston, Massachusetts, USA, where he taught deaf people, helping them learn to speak. Professor Bell, as he was called, also gave lectures and wrote research papers. Despite being very busy, he continued with his experiments to send voices via electricity.

The Bell home in Brantford, Canada

BELL HOMESTEAD

Bell Family Tree

Alexander Bell 1790–1865

Aleck's grandfather was a highly respected teacher of elocution in London. His work inspired the character of the elocution teacher, Henry Higgins, in the play *Pygmalion*, later made into the musical *My Fair Lady*.

Alexander Melville Bell 1819–1905

Aleck's father also taught elocution. He was particularly interested in teaching deaf people to speak. His system of written symbols called Visible Speech helped deaf people see how to make the sounds needed for speech.

———MARRIED———

Melville James Bell
1845–1870

Melville, Aleck's older brother, died of tuberculosis at age 25.

Alexander Graham Bell
1847–1922

Even as a child, Aleck tried to invent things. He was a curious boy and his parents encouraged his investigations. At age 16, Aleck started teaching elocution like his father and grandfather.

Aleck with his parents and brothers in Edinburgh, Scotland.

Eliza Grace Symonds Bell 1809–1897

Aleck's mother was a talented pianist and encouraged Aleck's interest in music. She began to lose her hearing when Aleck was 12 years old. Aleck's interest in his mother's deafness led to his investigation into sound waves.

Edward Charles Bell
1848–1867

Aleck's younger brother died of tuberculosis at age 19. Tuberculosis was a highly contagious disease of the lungs.

Bell Family Tree

The Bell family tree explains how Alexander Graham Bell's investigations into speech and sound were influenced by his parents and his paternal grandfather.

15

SOUND WAVES

Sounds are created when molecules vibrate. These vibrations, or sound waves, move through the air like ripples moving through water.

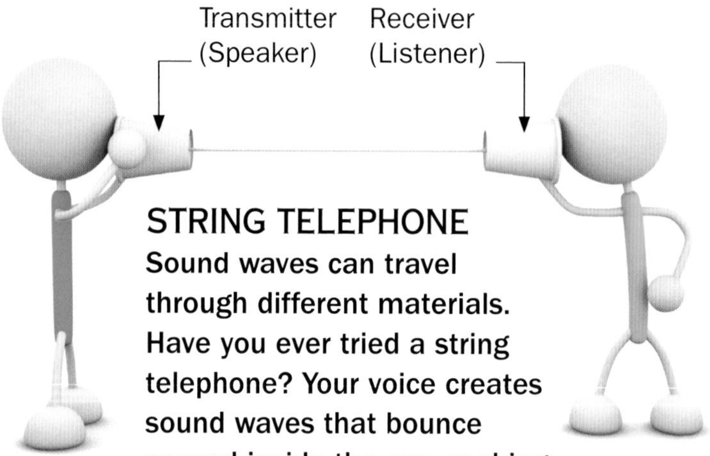

Transmitter (Speaker)

Receiver (Listener)

STRING TELEPHONE
Sound waves can travel through different materials. Have you ever tried a string telephone? Your voice creates sound waves that bounce around inside the cup, making the string vibrate. If the string is stretched tight, the sound waves can travel along it to the other end.

THE EFFECTS OF SOUND WAVES

You can't see sound waves in the air, but you can see their effects. Stretch some plastic wrap over a round cake tin. Hold it in place with an elastic band to make a drum. Sprinkle brown sugar onto the drum. Hold a baking tray close to the sugar without touching it. Now bang hard on the baking tray with a spoon!

1 When you bang the baking tray, it vibrates.

2 The vibrations send sound waves through the air.

3 When the sound waves reach the sugar, the sugar vibrates as well.

HEARING AND SPEAKING

Alexander Graham Bell was fascinated by how people hear and speak. His belief that vibrations, or sound waves, were key to both hearing and speaking led him to make some amazing discoveries.

HEARING SOUNDS

Sound waves travel through the outer ear canal and vibrate the eardrum, sending waves of pressure to the cochlea. This, in turn, sends signals to the hearing part of your brain, which interprets the sounds.

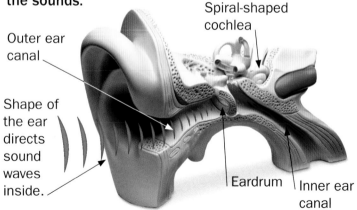

Spiral-shaped cochlea

Outer ear canal

Shape of the ear directs sound waves inside.

Eardrum

Inner ear canal

SPEAKING SOUNDS

Your voice box, or larynx, is located at the top of your windpipe. When you speak, you create a stream of air that causes two vocal cords in your larynx to vibrate, producing sound waves. You use your lips, tongue and cheeks to shape sounds into recognisable speech.

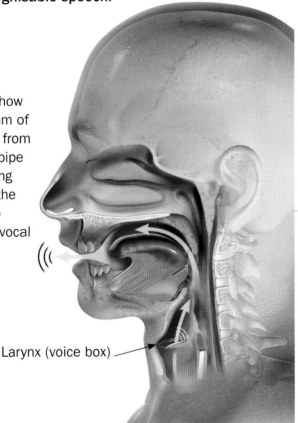

Arrows show the stream of air rising from the windpipe and exiting through the mouth to produce vocal sounds.

Larynx (voice box)

Sign Language

Sign language uses hands and fingers to communicate. Different sign languages are used around the world. Most use signs for an alphabet, and also for complete words.

AMERICAN SIGN LANGUAGE

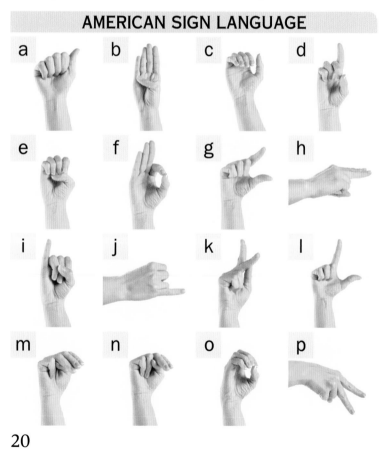

a

b

c

d

e

f

g

h

i

j

k

l

m

n

o

p

Use American Sign Language
to work out this word.

21

Visible Speech

Melville Bell, Aleck's father, developed a system of written symbols called Visible Speech that showed how to pronounce different sounds needed for speaking. Although deaf people could not hear the sounds themselves, they could look at the chart to see how to say the sounds.

MOUTH PARTS FOR SPEAKING

When you speak, you use different parts of your mouth, such as your lips, tongue, cheeks and teeth, to pronounce different sounds.

Diagram from a pamphlet for Visible Speech, 1872

HOW TO USE VISIBLE SPEECH
These are some symbols devised by
Melville Bell for Visible Speech.

Sound	How to use your mouth
	Put your lips together. Use your voice box as you open your mouth and breathe out.
	Same as for B, but don't use your voice box.
	Keep your lips together. Use your voice box and breathe out at the same time.
	Touch your tongue to the roof of the mouth. Use your voice box and breathe out at the same time.

INTERNATIONAL PHONETIC ALPHABET
Visible Speech formed the basis for today's
International Phonetic Alphabet (IPA), which is
used to learn pronunciation of foreign languages.

Chapter 1

WORKSHOP OF WILD DREAMS

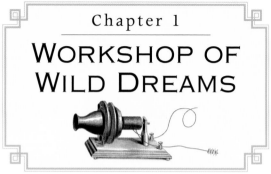

1874

As Aleck walked towards the centre of Boston, he noticed posters advertising the latest inventions. There were so many! The country was changing rapidly and business was booming, helped along by inventions such as the telegraph. Aleck turned onto Court Street, with its fine stone buildings, their grand shopfronts polished and gleaming. He crossed the busy street, dodging ponies and carts and horse-drawn carriages. Outside number 109, he looked up at the neat sign nailed in the stonework of the shop.

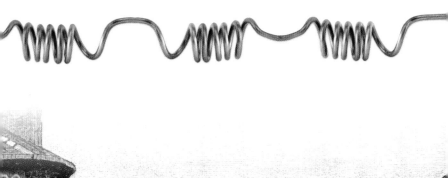

Court Street, Boston,
in the 1870s

Like many inventors, especially those working on electrical devices, Aleck had come to Charles Williams' shop not only to buy supplies but also for practical help with his inventions. Aleck had plenty of ideas, but he didn't have the skills necessary to make the devices that he had in his head.

He looked at the list of supplies he needed: wire, an electric battery, tuning forks, telegraph keys,

Copper wire

Tuning forks, usually used for musical instruments

Early battery called a 'hubble bubble'

sounders and registers. All of this equipment was going to cost a lot of money!

Aleck went inside and asked one of the electricians at the shop for help. Soon, Aleck and the electrician were deep in conversation about telegraphs and how to improve them. The electrician's name was Thomas Watson.

Aleck told Tom that he believed not only signals could be sent by wire, but also voices. In fact, he was working on a new invention to transmit voices called the telephone.

Tom didn't make fun of Aleck like other people sometimes did. He was interested in Aleck's idea. Tom had a talent for taking ideas and making them into working devices. He went to work with Aleck on his inventions. Together, Alexander Graham Bell and Thomas Watson were to change the world.

Aleck's brain was a constant buzz of ideas. He rented the attic rooms at 109 Court Street as a workshop, but he needed money for his experiments. Thomas Sanders and Gardiner Hubbard agreed to sponsor him. Sanders' young son, George, and Hubbard's teenage daughter, Mabel, were pupils of Aleck's. They respected him as a teacher of the deaf and liked his enthusiasm for inventing. If Aleck's inventions were successful, then they would become rich.

However, both Sanders and Hubbard thought that another of Aleck's ideas, a multiple telegraph, was their best chance for success – not the telephone.

Sanders told Aleck that the way to make their fortune was with a multiple telegraph that sent several messages all at the same time. He pointed out that when a customer spent a dollar on a telegram between New York and Chicago, the

Western Union company made a profit of 30 cents. Perhaps the multiple telegraph would eventually earn a profit like that! On the other hand, he thought Aleck's idea for a telephone was a far-fetched fantasy.

Thomas Sanders was investing a lot of money in the multiple telegraph and in this incredibly clever but rather wild young man. Sanders ran a profitable leather business and he felt he knew what would sell and what wouldn't. He also knew that he didn't want to lose his money on a crazy contraption like the telephone.

?

What words does the author use to convey that Aleck's telephone was considered a ridiculous idea?

TYPEWRITER

invented by Christopher Sholes in **1868**

Is your handwriting untidy?
Use a typewriter for professional-looking work.

**Press the keys of this amazing
typing machine. Using
the unique ink ribbon, the
typewriter actually prints onto
the paper as you type!**

As used by the author Mark Twain.

HENRY SEELY'S
ELECTRIC IRON
invented in 1882

**Tired of heating your iron
on the stove?**

Then the electric flatiron
is the solution for you!
(But you'll need a strong
arm – it's very heavy!)

30

EDISON'S

PHONOGRAPH

invented in 1877

A cylinder that sings!

Edison's phonograph is a whole show in itself. It can talk, sing or play beautiful music, depending on the cylinder you play. Just wind the handle and listen to the amazing sound. You'll never be lonely with an Edison phonograph for company!

Velocipede Bicycle
invented by Pierre Lallement
in 1866

Pedals – the latest development in two-wheeled fun! The faster you pedal, the faster you'll go. (The bike is made of heavy metal, so you'll have to pedal very hard to get anywhere.)

Investing in an Invention

Gardiner Hubbard

Aleck taught Hubbard's daughter, Mabel. Aleck felt strongly that deaf people like Mabel should be able to participate fully in a hearing world. Hubbard liked that. He also liked Aleck's ideas for inventions, so he invested in his work. As a lawyer, Hubbard helped Bell deal with the Patent Office – not an easy task. Nor were the controversies easy with Western Union.

Thomas Sanders

Aleck also taught Sanders' son, George. Sanders ran a profitable leather business. Although he did not usually invest his money in new inventions, he had a hunch that Aleck's multiple telegraph would be a success. Of all Aleck's inventions, that's the one that Sanders thought would make the biggest profit.

1 Alexander Graham Bell needed money to work on his inventions.

2 Gardiner Hubbard and Thomas Sanders gave him some money as an investment.

3 In return, Bell promised to share any money he made from his inventions.

4 Hubbard and Sanders were taking a risk. If Bell's inventions failed, they would lose the money that they had invested.

5 But if Bell's inventions became a success, they could make a big profit. (That means a lot of money!)

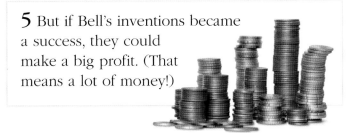

A Job for Tom Watson

Thomas Augustus Watson was born above a stable in Salem, Massachusetts, in 1854. His father was the foreman at the stable, but Tom did not share his father's interest in horses. He didn't particularly like school, either.

_____

At the age of 16, he got a job as a bookkeeper, keeping track of sales and purchases at a local business. He thought the job was boring. Next, he tried carpentry, making furniture out of wood. That didn't suit him either.

His real talent lay in making and designing machinery. Tom was fascinated by all the new gadgets being invented at the time. He became an electrician and machinist at the Williams Electrical  Shop at 109 Court Street, Boston, where he met many inventors who came to the shop for equipment.

One day at work, Tom met a young inventor named Alexander Graham Bell, who asked him to be his assistant. Tom liked working with Aleck. By all accounts, Aleck was refined and educated but could sometimes be a bit clumsy, while Tom was a cheerful, good-natured person who was good at practical things. They made an excellent team.

After helping Alexander Graham Bell invent the telephone, Tom went on to work in engineering, shipbuilding and education – and he even acted in Shakespearean plays! Tom Watson was a man of many interests.

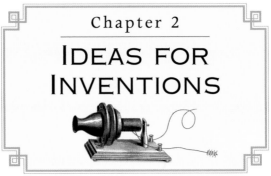

Chapter 2
IDEAS FOR INVENTIONS

FEBRUARY, 1875

Aleck ran upstairs to the attic workshop at 109 Court Street. Tom was already there. On the workbenches lay models, diagrams and notes on various inventions, including Aleck's ideas for the telephone, which he hoped would eventually transmit the human voice along an electric wire.

The invention on his mind at the moment was the telautograph. Tom held up the device he'd made according to Aleck's design. The telautograph wrote out telegraph messages using an attached pen. As the device received each signal, the pen automatically wrote the corresponding letter.

Aleck was delighted. It was just as he had imagined. His multiple telegraph was also coming along well. He called it a 'harmonic telegraph' because it used sound tones to send many signals at once.

Reconstruction of Aleck's workshop at 109 Court Street, Boston

The next day, Aleck planned to take the telautograph and harmonic telegraph to the United States Patent Office in Washington, D.C. He hoped that the Patent Office would recognise that these devices were real innovations. He needed a patent to say that the inventions were his and could not be copied by anyone else unless they paid for them.

Aleck hoped that no other inventors, such as Thomas Edison or Elisha Gray, had developed a harmonic telegraph like his that sent multiple messages.

Tom told him not to worry. Aleck's harmonic telegraph used sounds to transmit and receive many messages at once, while Edison's quadruplex telegraph could only take four messages at a time.

Aleck was glad that Tom had confidence in the harmonic telegraph.

He only wished his parents did, too. Although he sent them detailed notes on all his experiments, they disapproved of him spending so much time on his inventions. They thought that he should concentrate on teaching the deaf. They didn't seem to understand how his inventions and his teaching work were all part of the same thing. His teaching influenced his experiments and his experiments influenced his teaching.

At least the notes that he sent his parents would not be wasted. Mr Hubbard had instructed Aleck to save all of his notes and drawings because they might help him secure patents for his devices.

That evening, Tom stood by Aleck, working tirelessly. Squinting in the dim yellow light of the gas lamp, Tom fixed the telautograph's transmitter to the wooden base.

The telautograph was a curious device. Aleck had been inspired by a real human ear. He'd used the ear to develop a different device to help deaf students measure how well they could speak.

Aleck's design had a mouthpiece that channelled his voice to the eardrum of the human ear. The sound waves from his voice made the small bones of the inner ear vibrate onto a piece of straw that he had attached to the bones. The straw then scratched a series of visible waves onto a glass plate that was coated in dusty grey charcoal.

Although his deaf students couldn't hear themselves speak, they could see the wave patterns that their speech made on the glass and try to match them to Aleck's. The closer their wave patterns were to Aleck's, the closer their speech was, too.

If sound could cause the piece of straw to vibrate, then Aleck was sure that it could also cause an electric current to vibrate. Then he would be able to transmit voices over a telephone.

The force of a voice would move the electric current. By tuning the current to different frequencies of sound, all the tones in the voice would be transmitted along a single wire. They would be able to send human speech as far and as fast as electricity could take it – even to the ends of the world!

Suddenly, Aleck and Tom were startled by a sound at the door. It was Gardiner Hubbard, one of Aleck's sponsors.

He didn't approve of Aleck spending his time experimenting with the telephone. He laughed at the idea of sending human speech to the ends of the world. Why couldn't Aleck just concentrate on the harmonic telegraph?

Aleck felt weak at the knees, partly from nervousness, but also from hunger. He often forgot to eat. When he did remember, he sometimes had to borrow money from Tom in order to buy food. Most of his money went to pay for supplies for his inventions.

Aleck knew that Mr Hubbard thought sending speech over a wire was simply impossible. After all, Antonio Meucci of Italy had filed a similar idea with the Patent Office in 1871. It used the same basic theories as Aleck's telephone.

However, Meucci only filed the idea –
the caveat – not a full patent for the
design. He never renewed the caveat
or proceeded with the full patent
application. Hubbard thought this
was because it couldn't be done.
Aleck thought differently.

Antonio Meucci

Gardiner Hubbard was a highly regarded patent lawyer and was certain that Aleck's harmonic telegraph and telautograph had by far the best chance of success. As one of Aleck's main sponsors, Hubbard also provided him with the money to do his experiments. Aleck needed his support.

Hubbard was to accompany Aleck to the Patent Office in Washington, D.C. the following day. He had come to make sure that the harmonic telegraph and telautograph were ready.

United States Patent Office, Washington, D.C.

Yes, they were ready, and of course Aleck was hopeful that they'd be granted patents. Yet he couldn't help dwelling on the telephone. He had a hunch that it would be his most important invention – but he and Tom had a lot of work to do before he could even submit a patent application.

?

Why did Aleck feel pressured to work on the harmonic telegraph and the telautograph rather than the telephone?

Patent Office
Instruction Leaflet

Applying for a patent

If you have invented a new product or have improved on an existing product, then you will need to apply for a government patent. The patent will protect your invention so other people cannot make, sell or use it without your permission.

> **Note:** A patent may be held by an individual or by a company. The patent holder may also decide to sell the patent rights to another individual or company.
>
> **The patent covers:**
> - ⋆ what your invention does
> - ⋆ how your invention is made
> - ⋆ materials used
> - ⋆ how your invention works

How do I apply for a patent?

1 **Complete a written patent application from the Patent Office.**
2 **Explain how to make your invention, including materials used.**
3 **Detail how to use your invention.**
4 **Include drawings, diagrams and measurements.**
5 **Send your application to the Patent Office with the fee.**
6 **Wait for the verdict. Has your patent been granted?**

Each country currently has its own patent laws, although the World Trade Organisation is trying to standardise patent rules to make them more international.

Note: Your patent will have to be renewed after a specified number of years.

Note: In the UK, you should apply for a patent from the Intellectual Property Office (IPO), which recommends hiring a patent attorney or other professional advisor to assist you.

Chapter 3
GOOD NEWS AND BAD NEWS

MARCH, 1875

Patent applications and caveats for all sorts of new gadgets poured in to the United States Patent Office in Washington, D.C. While Aleck waited for news about his harmonic telegraph and telautograph, he arranged to show his latest telephone model to Professor Joseph Henry of the Smithsonian Institution. Professor Henry was a distinguished scientist who had invented the electromagnet, a key part of Aleck's idea for the telephone. Aleck had great admiration for him.

Now Aleck looked up at the newly built Smithsonian Institution. Set in a vast park in Washington, the towering turrets made the building look like a castle.

Smithsonian Institution in Washington, D.C.

Inside, Aleck nervously set up his telephone equipment in the Professor's wood-panelled study. Carefully, he connected it together exactly as he and Tom Watson had done in their attic workshop. Professor Henry observed closely.

Professor
Joseph
Henry

Eng ᵈ by Geo. E. Perine, N.Y.

Then he held the coil of wire against his ear and listened for what seemed to Aleck to be a very long time.

Later, Aleck wrote to his parents, "He [Professor Henry] said he thought it was 'the germ of a great invention'... I cannot tell you how much these...words have encouraged me."

Aleck returned to Boston feeling much more positive. He told Tom that the great Joseph Henry thought the telephone was worth pursuing. They were determined to continue with their experiments.

Listening to muffled sounds was a world away from hearing the spoken word, but it was a start. Both Aleck and Professor Henry recognised that there was much more to do before a full working machine could be developed. Nevertheless, Aleck felt certain that with his own skills and the skills of Tom Watson, they would find a solution.

Later in March, 1875

However, Thomas Sanders and Gardiner Hubbard were still sure that the harmonic telegraph was the key to fame and fortune. Both men had invested a lot in Aleck and wanted profits in return. In fact, Thomas Sanders was beginning to run out of money and he was afraid he might lose his home and his business.

So when Aleck received an invitation to demonstrate his harmonic telegraph to the mighty Western Union, he simply could not refuse. If he could sell his improved technology to the biggest telegraph company in the world, they would all benefit.

This time, Aleck took the train to New York City. In the dim grey light of early evening, he walked towards the bright lights that shone from the windows of the 70-metre (230-ft) tall Western Union building. Completed earlier that year,

it was one of the tallest buildings in New York City. This modern new building was a symbol of the enormous power and potential of the communications industry.

Aleck strode through the grand doors and into the steam-driven elevator, marvelling at the fact that he, Aleck Bell, had been invited here to demonstrate his invention. Of course, being Aleck, he also wondered if electricity would be a better way of powering the elevator.

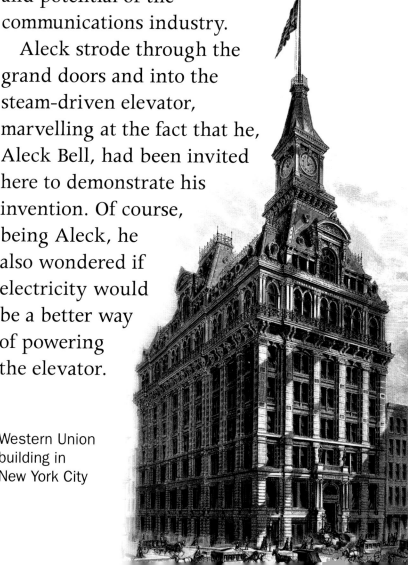

Western Union building in New York City

The elevator stopped and the elevator boy pulled open the door. A man waiting in the corridor introduced himself to Aleck. He was George Prescott, Chief Electrician for Western Union.

Aleck followed him to the Western Union testing laboratory, which was far more spacious and well equipped than his workshop in Boston. Using two electromagnetic transmitters, Aleck set up two channels that ran simultaneously.

Prescott watched as the signals went back and forth. The signals seemed to be fairly clear, and they were fast enough. Aleck proudly pointed out that if two electromagnetic transmitters worked smoothly along one wire, then there could be many more!

Prescott suggested trying the harmonic telegraph on a longer route – to Philadelphia, 153 km (95 miles) away.

The message transmitted perfectly to the Western Union office in Philadelphia. They sent a message back to New York, which was also received clearly.

Prescott was impressed, but said that the electromagnets were a little weak. They agreed to try the harmonic telegraph with stronger electromagnets. While Prescott sent off for the best and strongest electromagnets that only Western Union could provide, Aleck went home and waited impatiently.

?

What was Aleck hoping to achieve by demonstrating his harmonic telegraph at Western Union?

Instead of being invited back for more testing, Aleck was summoned to meet with William Orton, the powerful president of Western Union.

Aleck expected Orton to offer him a huge sum of money for his harmonic telegraph. After all, Western Union would need thousands of devices to equip their offices across the country. Aleck would be rich! The money would enable him to focus on his favorite invention – the telephone.

Then the blow came.

Orton said he had two problems. The first was that Elisha Gray's multiple telegraph was similar to Aleck's. Because Gray was chief engineer of Western Electric Manufacturing Company, Orton trusted his skills over Aleck's.

Then Orton explained his second problem – that he didn't like Aleck's sponsor, Gardiner Hubbard. Orton refused to do business with Hubbard or his associates, including Aleck. He had therefore chosen the multiple telegraph invented by Elisha Gray.

Orton stood up to indicate that the meeting was over. Aleck left Western Union in a daze. As he walked back out to the busy New York streets, his dream was in tatters.

Outside the Western Union building in New York City

Aleck met Gardiner Hubbard at the famous Delmonico's Restaurant in New York City. Despite the glamorous surroundings, their mood was sombre.

Delmonico's Restaurant in Manhattan, New York City

Hubbard told Aleck that he had sent several letters of complaint about Western Union's tight grip on the telegraph industry. He didn't like Western Union, and William Orton knew it. Since the telegraph giant had no competition, Hubbard felt they could do as they pleased without regard for their customers. He'd even sent letters of complaint about Western Union to the United States government!

Hubbard sighed and told Aleck that he thought this was Western Union's way of getting back at him.

Aleck was furious. The following morning, he put aside his usual mild manners and stormed into Western Union's plush building. He was no longer impressed by its grandeur. He rode the elevator upstairs and marched straight into the vast laboratory to get his equipment back.

ELECTROMAGNETS

Bell's telephone relied on electromagnets, whose power could be turned on and off by an electric current. Today, we use electromagnets for a wide variety of uses.

Man uses a 'butter stamp' telephone.

Wires carry the electric current.

ELECTRICITY + MAGNETISM
The link between electricity and magnets was proven in 1820 by Danish scientist Hans Christian Oersted. When he brought a compass near a wire carrying an electric current, the needle on the compass moved. This showed that an electric current produces a magnetic field.

ELECTROMAGNETIC DISCOVERIES
In the 1830s, American scientist Joseph Henry and British scientist Michael Faraday discovered that a magnetic field can also produce electricity. Aleck used this effect, called electromagnetic induction, in the telephone.

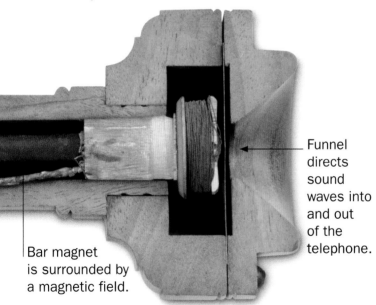

Funnel directs sound waves into and out of the telephone.

Bar magnet is surrounded by a magnetic field.

ELECTROMAGNETISM IN THE TELEPHONE
In both the transmitter and receiver, the magnetic field of the bar magnet varies, which in turn produces varying electric currents.

MAKE AN ELECTROMAGNET

Electricity can create magnetism. Unlike ordinary magnets, the power of an electromagnet can be switched on and off by an electric current. Electromagnetism has a wide range of uses, from electric motors and generators to doorbells and, of course, telephones.

You will need:

copper wire

9-volt battery

paper clips

adhesive tape

screwdriver with plastic handle

1 Wind the copper wire tightly around the middle of the screwdriver as shown. Use tape to secure the wire at each end.

2 Connect both ends of the wire to the battery. The screwdriver will now become magnetised. (Be careful – the wire may be hot!)

3 You can now use your screwdriver electromagnet to pick up paper clips and other objects made from magnetic materials. The more times you wind the wire, the stronger the magnetic field will be.

Attach both ends of the wire to the battery terminals.

Screwdriver handle

Copper wire

Screwdriver end

Paper clips

4 When you disconnect the screwdriver electromagnet from the battery, it will start to lose its magnetism and drop whatever it is holding.

63

WESTERN UNION
Timeline

1851 Western Union is founded as the New York and Mississippi Valley Printing Telegraph Company.

1856 Merges with other telegraph lines in the western United States and changes its name to Western Union.

1890s Begins transmitting telegrams around the world.

1800

1861 Opens first transcontinental telegraph line across North America.

1871 Introduces money transfers, which later become the main business.

Although it started as a telegraph company, Western Union is now better known for enabling customers to send and receive money almost anywhere in the world.

1933 First singing telegram

1980 Business focus of Western Union changes when money transfers overtake the telegram business.

1900　　　　　　　　　　　　　　　**2000**

1974 Launches first American commercial satellite into space.

2000s Now customers can transfer money via the internet, mobile phones and even bank machines.

65

Chapter 4
MAKING CONNECTIONS

6TH APRIL, 1875

Aleck was in low spirits after his experience with Western Union. Finding time for both teaching and inventing was hard work, but he was determined.

Exactly one month after submitting his patent application for the telautograph and the harmonic telegraph, Aleck received a response.

Clutching his letter, he walked briskly along Court Street to number 85, where he was due to meet Gardiner Hubbard at the Oriental Tea Company's Store. Aleck had not been to the Tea Company before.

Glass lamps lit the dark wood surfaces where people sipped warm tea. A sign announced that customers could buy their favourite teas to take home, from the smoky Chinese Lap Sang Souchong to the perfumed, musky Indian Darjeeling.

Aleck thought how lucky he was to live in the city of Boston, with its links across the vast oceans lapping its shores. One day, perhaps, his talking machines might make those links shorter.

Gardiner Hubbard sat at the far end of a row of chairs set against a wall of paintings. He motioned for Aleck to sit. Aleck handed him the letter.

It wasn't the news they had hoped for. The Patent Office had only granted Aleck a patent for the telautograph, but not for the harmonic telegraph.

Through his contacts at the Patent Office, Gardiner Hubbard had found out that they were holding back on the patent for the harmonic telegraph. Elisha Gray, among others, had filed a similar patent application, and the Patent Office wanted to study them all carefully. They had to decide which invention was the best – and who was first.

Elisha Gray

May, 1875

Aleck tried to push the recent disappointments to the back of his mind as he and Tom continued their experiments on the telephone.

He had a theory for transmitting speech. Thanks to his experience in speech and elocution, he knew that voice tones rise and fall by varying degrees. An electric current must also vary in order for the voice tones to be heard. Aleck's idea was to use steel reeds that vibrated according to different tones.

Aleck and Tom persevered with the telephone, trying many different experiments with no luck. Tom wrote later, "Its operation was so uncertain and baffling that I remember even Professor Bell himself began to lose enthusiasm."

But they did not give up. Then, one hot summer's day, they made an important breakthrough….

2ND JUNE, 1875

The attic rooms on Court Street were particularly hot and sticky. Aleck mopped his brow. Sometimes he wished their workshop was in the cool basement instead of high up in the attic! It was freezing in the attic in winter and sweltering in summer. What was more, the dampness created havoc with the electrical contacts.

Aleck shouted loudly so Tom could hear him in the next room. Tom called back to tell Aleck that he was just tuning the transmitter reeds so they were each on the right frequency.

Aleck was ready. He pressed the receiver to his ear. At that moment, Tom noticed that a reed on the transmitter was not vibrating as it should, so he plucked it.

TWAAAANNGG!

Aleck heard the twanging of the reed. To his astonishment, the sound was coming through the receiver! What was more, he could hear several tones coming from the receiver, just like the tones of the tuning forks he had experimented with in his youth.

"Mr. Watson!" he called. "Mr. Watson! Please make that reed twang again!"

Tom plucked the reed, again and again. Each time, Aleck heard the twanging of the reed through the receiver. There was no mistaking it.

Bell's first telephone

"We've done it, Mr. Watson!" Aleck shouted, running into the room next door. "I have heard the first real sound to be transmitted electrically!"

Aleck reasoned that the reed's vibrations must have created a current in the electromagnet, which ran all the way along the wire to the receiver where he had heard the musical tones. If a plucked reed could vibrate and be heard as musical tones, then so could words – and even voices!

Aleck wrote a letter to Gardiner Hubbard, saying, "I have accidentally made a discovery of the very greatest importance in regard to Transmitting Instruments."

"We spent the rest of the day repeating the experiment," said Tom later. "...Then Bell sketched out the first speaking telephone the world has ever seen and gave me instructions for its construction...."

Now they needed to improve the telephone so voices could be heard clearly.

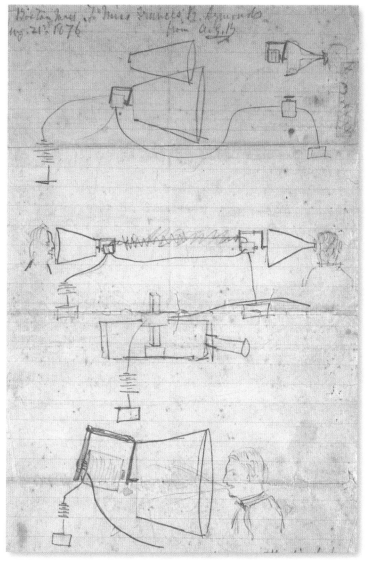

Aleck's sketch of the first speaking telephone

1st July, 1875

However, there was no further progress for several weeks. Aleck and Tom experimented with different adjustments to the telephone, but the sounds they heard through the receiver did not get any clearer.

Then they tested a new model. Aleck stayed up in the attic with the transmitter, while Tom took the receiver downstairs. Tom had attached a 91-metre (300-ft) wire, so the test would be a tough one.

Upstairs, Aleck shouted and sang down the transmitter.

Transmitter

Receiver

Downstairs, Tom listened intently.
Then he shot back upstairs.

"I can hear your voice quite plainly,
Mr Bell!" he declared. "I can almost
make out what you said!"

?

Why was the telephone tested
on 1st July, 1875 such
a big improvement?

A delighted Aleck wrote to his father to tell him the news. "The varying pitch of the voice was plainly discernible at the other end of the line," he wrote. "I feel that I am on the threshold of a great discovery."

Aleck wrote to Thomas Sanders and Gardiner Hubbard, too. They were still encouraging him to concentrate on the harmonic telegraph, but perhaps now they would also support his work on the telephone.

Aleck had another reason for wanting Hubbard's backing. He had fallen in love with Hubbard's daughter, Mabel, one of his deaf students. Aleck liked her sense of adventure and admired her determination.

However, as a polite young man, he was waiting for her father's permission before declaring his love. He would also need enough money to support a wife

and family before considering marriage.

Mabel Hubbard had given Aleck a small crumb of hope in one of her recent letters. "If you ever need my friendly help and sympathy, it is yours," she had written.

Would she ever be more than a friend to Aleck?

Transcript of excerpt of letter

Dear Mr Bell

Thank you very much for the honourable and generous way in which you have treated me. Indeed you have both my respect and esteem. I shall be glad to see you in Cambridge and become better acquainted with you.

Letter from Mabel to Aleck, August 1875

Early Telephones

Bell's telephone was the start of a revolutionary new form of communication that would have an enormous impact on people's lives.

An actor playing Alexander Graham Bell re-enacts the famous inventor speaking into one of his early telephones.

Transmitter

EARLY TELEPHONE

HOW A TELEPHONE WORKS

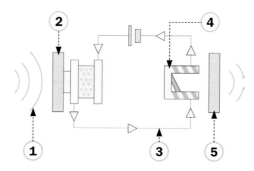

1 Sound waves from the caller's voice vibrate a flexible disk, or diaphragm, in the transmitter.

2 The diaphragm turns the sound waves into varying electrical signals.

3 The electrical signals travel along the phone line to the receiver.

4 An electromagnet in the receiver turns the varying electrical signals back into sound waves.

5 The sound waves make the diaphragm in the receiver vibrate, reproducing the caller's voice.

Receiver

Mabel Hubbard

Mabel was born in 1857. She lost her hearing after a serious bout of scarlet fever when she was a little girl.

Mabel in 1877, the year she married Alexander Graham Bell. That year, they travelled to England to demonstrate Aleck's telephone for Queen Victoria. Mabel shared Aleck's interest in science and encouraged his experiments.

Mabel and Aleck Bell and their two daughters, Elsie (left) and Marian, who was called Daisy.

In the early 1900s, Mabel and Aleck became interested in the idea of flying machines. Here, Mabel flies a tetrahedral kite, invented by Aleck.

Mabel and Aleck in their later years, taken in the grounds of their home in Nova Scotia, Canada.

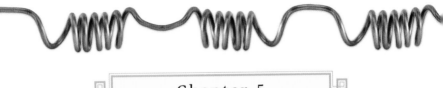

Chapter 5

THE RACE FOR THE PATENT

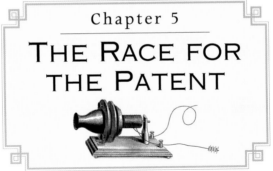

26TH NOVEMBER, 1875

As Aleck stepped out of 109 Court Street, his breath turned to fog in the wintry air. Boston was having a cold spell. Yesterday had been the coldest Thanksgiving Day on record.

Aleck wrapped his scarf around his neck as he headed for downtown Boston. He grinned. Cold weather wouldn't bother him. After all, he had grown up in Scotland and lived in Canada. In fact, nothing at all bothered him today.

To Aleck's delight, Mabel Hubbard had agreed to marry him! Yesterday,

on her 18th birthday, they had become officially engaged. Thankfully, her father no longer objected.

Now, if only Aleck's parents would stop asking him to give up his experiments. If only Mr Hubbard and Mr Sanders would stop asking him to give up his work on the telephone. If only his harmonic telegraph would succeed so he could make some money and marry Mabel!

Boston in the winter

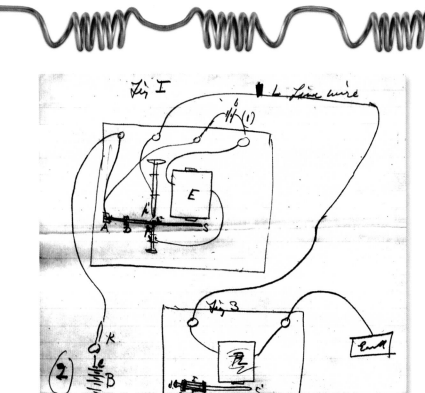
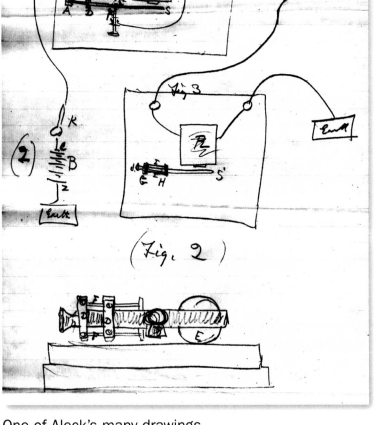

One of Aleck's many drawings

84

Aleck was ignoring the advice of his parents and sponsors. Progress on both the harmonic telegraph and the telephone had been so vast and so quick that he intended to take his designs to the Patent Office again – but Tom had highlighted a problem.

Their drawings didn't look very professional. They needed a properly trained draughtsman to make clear, detailed technical drawings. Then the examiners at the Patent Office might take them more seriously.

On this cold, blustery day, Aleck was on his way to downtown Boston to meet Lewis Latimer. Mr Latimer was a respected draughtsman for a patent law firm who advised hopeful inventors.

Aleck swung open the door of the coffee house and spotted Mr Latimer, a well-dressed young African American, already sitting at a table.

Latimer had a reputation for working harder than everyone else, being more eager, and working later into the night. He had quickly progressed from office boy to head draughtsman – and he had some inventions of his own as well.

So, how could he help Aleck?

Using his set squares, protractors and compasses, Latimer declared that he would transform Aleck's sketches into professional technical drawings. Aleck could see that this made sense. The clearer and more detailed his applications to the Patent Office, the better his chances of success.

So Aleck began the first of many useful meetings with Lewis Latimer. Aleck showed Latimer his rough diagrams and explained his ideas, and the professional draughtsman drew them into neat, clear and detailed designs.

Draughtsman's tools of a set square and compass

14TH FEBRUARY, 1876

Aleck was careful, too, to write down his experiments in a more logical, professional way. He carefully explained his latest development of a variable resistance liquid transmitter to transport the voice over a varying current. Then on Valentine's Day, 1876, he submitted an application to the United States Patent Office for the telephone.

Aleck's rival, Elisha Gray, submitted a caveat to the Patent Office on the very same day, only two hours after Aleck – and Gray also used a liquid transmitter!

29TH FEBRUARY, 1876

At the end of February, Aleck's lawyer summoned him to come to Washington, D.C. He recommended that Aleck meet with Zenas F. Wilber, the Examiner for the United States Patent Office, to discuss his patent application.

It was Mr Wilber's job to inspect the patent applications and decide which inventions were genuinely new ideas. Luckily for Aleck, he was taking a particular interest in the race to improve the telegraph.

Mr Wilber confirmed that the Patent Office had received Aleck's application. However, they had also received at least four similar applications, including one from Elisha Gray, another from Thomas Edison – and even one sent from across the ocean in Copenhagen, Denmark!

Aleck was astonished. Gardiner Hubbard had told him that competition for patents could be fierce, but this was unbelievable!

Nevertheless, he refused to give up, especially not when he was so close. Aleck carefully explained every detail of his patent application to Mr Wilber. He also had lots of notes and diagrams to back up his case.

Aleck wrote to his father that night, "You can hardly understand the state of uncertainty and suspense in which I am now. The result of this application will affect my life in some way or other.... Should it succeed I know that fortune would be the reward of perseverance."

?

Why is a patent so important to inventors?

The Life of Lewis Latimer

·✲·

1848–1928

Born

4th September, 1848

Background

Lewis Howard Latimer was the youngest of four children of George and Rebecca Latimer. His parents had escaped from slavery in Virginia and moved north to Boston.

Education

Although Lewis only attended school for a few years, he enjoyed reading, writing stories and drawing.

American Civil War

At age 16, Lewis joined the Union Navy to help fight slavery during the American Civil War (1861–1865).

Draughting Career

After the war, Lewis became an office boy at a patent law firm in Boston. He was fascinated by the draughtsmen's precise diagrams of new inventions. He taught himself the skill of draughting and was promoted to Chief Draughtsman. He drew the diagrams for Alexander Graham Bell's 1876 patent application for the telephone.

Helping to Light the World

Lewis then turned his attention to the incandescent electric light bulb, which had just been invented by Thomas Edison. He created a process for manufacturing carbon filaments for electric light bulbs. Lewis supervised the installation of lighting systems in several major cities in the US, Canada and Europe. Later, he had the honour of becoming one of the 28 original Edison Pioneers.

Inventions

· Brighter and more durable light bulb filaments
· Threaded wooden socket for light bulbs
· Improved toilets on trains
· Safety elevator
· Lockable hat and coat rack
· Early air conditioner

Publications

Incandescent Electric Lighting: A Practical Description of the Edison System (published 1890)

Family

Married Mary Wilson; two daughters, Jeanette and Louise.

Hobbies and Interests

· Lewis enjoyed reading, writing poetry and plays, drawing and painting, and playing the flute.
· He taught English, drawing and draughting to immigrants who settled in the United States from other countries.
· He campaigned for the rights of African Americans.

Here are examples of job advertisements from Aleck's time, and today. How has the job of a draughtsperson changed?

Draughtsman
wanted

Draughtsman wanted to work with inventor who needs professional technical drawings of inventions.
Drawings must be clearly understood
by examiners at the Patent Office.

The job applicant must:

☞ use the information given by the inventor to make accurate drawings of each device

☞ have experience of drawing three-dimensional objects

☞ be skilled in using rulers, set squares and compasses

☞ have both mechanical and electrical knowledge

☞ be able to make precise scale drawings

☞ demonstrate attention to detail

Junior Draughtsperson required

Position available on a team with engineers and designers working on digital devices such as mobile phones and music players.

The job applicant must:

- use the information given by engineers and designers to make accurate drawings

- be trained in Computer Aided Design (CAD) software to make precise scale drawings

- have knowledge of electrical circuitry

- be skilled in using calculators, mathematical tables and technical handbooks, as well as rulers, set squares and compasses

- demonstrate attention to detail

- work well as part of a team

Computer Aided Design
Today, 'inventing' is often called 'product design' and technical drawings are done using computer-aided design (CAD) software. Draughtspeople can do technical drawings on the computer, rotate the image to view it from different angles and make changes on screen.

Chapter 6
THE SOUND OF SUCCESS

3RD MARCH, 1876

At long last, the Patent Office granted the telephone patent to Aleck! He received official notification of his patent on 3rd March, 1876, his 29th birthday.

Mr Wilber had pointed out the particularly close similarities between Aleck's application and Elisha Gray's submissions, which were sponsored by Western Union. His main concern was that both inventors used a variable resistance liquid transmitter. Luckily, Aleck was able to prove that his paperwork had been filed first.

"I am so glad you have at last obtained this patent for which you have worked so hard and have now, as you say, a fair prospect of success," wrote Mabel in her letter of congratulations. "Is it not nice that your patent should come so like a birthday present."

Now that he had the patent, Aleck put his mind towards achieving his next goal. After all, if his telephone was to have 'a fair prospect of success', it needed to transmit clear, unmistakable words. Could he do it?

?

Aleck was a very determined and persistent person. What do the words 'determined' and 'persistent' mean?

7TH MARCH, 1876

Aleck came bounding up the stairs of 109 Court Street, waving a large envelope. Inside was his patent certificate for the telephone!

Patent number 174,465, granted for Aleck's telephone, turned out to be one of the most important patents ever. At long last, Aleck also received the patent for his harmonic telegraph, but even his sponsors now recognised that the telephone had more potential.

Mabel was overjoyed for Aleck, and also for her father. Gardiner Hubbard had suffered many setbacks because of William Orton, president of the mighty Western Union. Now, though, it seemed as if Aleck had defeated Mr Orton, and his own rival, Elisha Gray.

With Tom's help, Aleck set to work on the next task, because they still didn't hear voices down the telephone any better than before. What was the point of the telephone unless they could hear words clearly?

Aleck and Tom decided to set up their new experiments at Aleck's apartment at 5 Exeter Place nearby. It was there that they forged ahead with their idea for sending words through a liquid transmitter.

?

Why do you think Aleck's patent for the telephone was one of the most important patents ever?

10TH MARCH, 1876

A few days later, something incredible happened at Exeter Place. Aleck described it in a letter to his parents.

"I was in one room at the Transmitting Instrument and Mr Watson at the Receiving Instrument – out of earshot. I called out into the Transmitting Instrument, 'Mr Watson – come here – I want to see you!' And he came! He said he had heard every word perfectly distinctly come from the electromagnet at the other end."

Aleck and Tom changed places. Tom sang into the transmitter. Then he read from a book. Aleck could hear him through the receiver, although the sound was a bit muffled.

"The last sentence however, I heard very plainly and distinctly," wrote Aleck. "It was, 'Mr Bell, do you understand what I say?' This is a great day for me.

I feel that I have at last struck the solution to a great problem."

It was an important moment, but without any fuss, the two men quietly took notes on the workings and success of their new transmitter. And so, the first true telephone was born without any fanfare at all.

Model of telephone transmitter that sent the famous first words, "Mr Watson – come here – I want to see you!"

Aleck's sponsors finally agreed that the telephone had a bright future ahead. What they needed now was publicity. On 25th May, 1876, Aleck publicly demonstrated the telephone for the first time at the Massachusetts Institute of Technology. Unfortunately, not many people took notice.

Gardiner Hubbard urged him to exhibit his telephone at the International Centennial Exhibition in Philadelphia. This was a special event celebrating 100 years since the United States had declared independence. Along with the public, there would be many respected scientists attending. There would also be a competition for the best invention.

Among the distinguished judges was Sir William Thompson (also known as Lord Kelvin), the British scientist who had supervised the transatlantic telegraph cable. Also in attendance

was Dom Pedro, the Emperor of Brazil, who had a strong interest in science and education. Aleck had met Dom Pedro during the emperor's recent visit to The Boston School for the Deaf.

However, Aleck was very busy with his teaching. He'd planned to attend the Exhibition at a later date to demonstrate Visible Speech, but a very determined Mabel persuaded him that he must go now! She even bought his railway ticket and made sure he boarded the train. Aleck did not regret it.

25TH JUNE, 1876

At the exhibition, Elisha Gray, sponsored by Western Union, was on the exhibition stage demonstrating his version of the harmonic telegraph. As he played music into a transmitter 91 metres (300 ft) away, the notes of *Home Sweet Home* rang out through the receiver that was on the stage. The audience and judges gasped in surprise!

How could Aleck compete? He had a small exhibit of his telephone equipment, but some of it had broken on the train and he'd had to fix it as best he could. In any case, no one was paying him much attention. Aleck was hot and sweaty – there was a heat wave in Philadelphia. He just wanted to go home.

"There were about 50 persons present," Aleck later wrote to his parents. "The Emperor and Sir William sat in the centre. Presently, Dom Pedro, in glancing around, caught sight of me and recognised me as having been introduced to him in Boston.

When Gray's exhibit was over, Dom Pedro came up to me and shook hands.... Sir William and Dom Pedro then came to see my apparatus. I then went into a different room and sang into the telephone."

Poster from the Centennial Exhibition, 1876

Aleck's letter continued: "Sir William listened and heard my voice distinctly. I articulated a sentence, 'Do you hear what I say?'

He listened and said, 'Yes – do you – understand – what I say?' He requested me to sing and recite something.

The Emperor then listened and exclaimed in surprise…'I have heard – I have heard!'

Some others present also listened…. Indeed it was a great and glorious success."

Even Elisha Gray had heard the voices on the telephone, loud and clear!

So what was the final outcome? Elisha Gray received a prize for his version of the harmonic telegraph. Aleck triumphed by winning one for Visible Speech – and another for the telephone.

The media were still unimpressed, but this soon changed. On 9th October of that same year, Tom and Aleck set up the first two-way telephone conversation on a 3.2-kilometre (2-mile) stretch of telegraph wire. This time, the Boston newspapers reported their achievement. The news spread around the country and beyond. Alexander Graham Bell and the telephone had arrived.

This picture shows how use of the telephone spread.

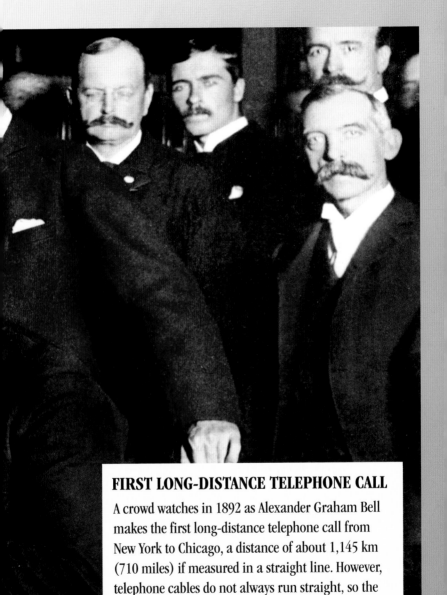

FIRST LONG-DISTANCE TELEPHONE CALL

A crowd watches in 1892 as Alexander Graham Bell makes the first long-distance telephone call from New York to Chicago, a distance of about 1,145 km (710 miles) if measured in a straight line. However, telephone cables do not always run straight, so the actual distance was even longer.

107

Ringing the Changes

Once news of Aleck's invention spread, he was in demand to demonstrate his telephone. Here, he fascinates spectators in Boston in 1877. Aleck was accustomed to public speaking from his years of teaching elocution and demonstrating Visible Speech.

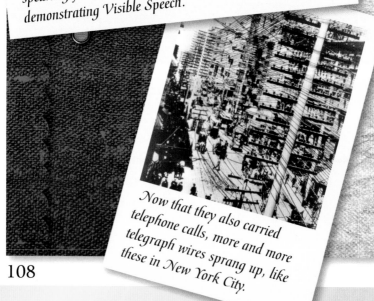

Now that they also carried telephone calls, more and more telegraph wires sprang up, like these in New York City.

Many telephone operators were needed to connect calls. This provided new job opportunities for women in the late 1800s. These telephone operators put through calls at an exchange in Madrid, Spain.

The telephone meant that people could speak to each other directly across long distances. It was ideal for businesspeople and also ordinary people. Friends could have a chat over the phone and couples could flirt – or even propose marriage as this cartoon shows!

Quotes by
Alexander Graham Bell

"The day will come when the man at the telephone will be able to see the distant person to whom he is speaking."

"The day is coming when telegraph wires will be laid onto houses just like water or gas – and friends converse with each other without leaving home."

About the
telephone

"Sometimes we stare so long at a door that is closing that we see too late the one that is open."

"Don't keep forever on the public road, going only where others have gone…. Leave the beaten track occasionally and dive into the woods. Every time you do so, you will be certain to find something that you have never seen before."

Have courage
to try new things

"Concentrate all your thoughts upon the work at hand. The sun's rays do not burn until brought to a focus."

The keys to success

"Before anything else, preparation is the key to success."

"Great discoveries and improvements invariably involve the cooperation of many minds."

"The most successful men in the end are those whose success is the result of steady accretion." (In other words – success happens one step at a time.)

TELEPHONES RING

Aleck and Tom – along with Mabel, her father, Gardiner Hubbard, and Thomas Sanders – offered the telephone invention to Western Union for $100,000. Despite their dislike of the company, they thought the telegraph giant would be the logical partner to invest in the next big step in the communications industry. However, William Orton turned down the deal. It was one of the biggest business mistakes in history.

Instead, Aleck and the others set up the Bell Telephone Company in 1877. But Aleck didn't like business. In 1880, he won a large prize set up by Alessandro Volta, the French inventor of the battery. He sold his share in Bell Telephone Company and built the Volta Laboratory in Washington, D.C. Here, with wife Mabel, he continued his experiments.

He researched sound and ways for deaf people to communicate. His many inventions included a metal detector, a hydrofoil for travelling on water and a photophone that ran along a beam of light. He was also involved with *Science* magazine and *National Geographic*.

Tom Watson continued to improve the telephone, along with other inventors such as Thomas Edison. In 1881, he left the Bell Telephone Company and set up an engineering workshop. He built ships and took a strong interest in education and schools for the future. With Aleck's encouragement, he also studied voice and drama. Tom enjoyed trying new experiences.

On 25th January, 1915, Aleck made the first transcontinental telephone call from New York City on the East Coast of the United States to San Francisco, California, on the West Coast. Aleck's voice travelled along the cable for several thousand kilometres. His old friend and colleague, Tom Watson, was in San Francisco to receive the call.

The debate about the patent goes on. Meucci and Gray's contributions to the telephone have now also been officially recognised. We can learn an important lesson from the story of the telephone: always write careful notes; make neat, detailed diagrams; and keep it all! If Aleck had not done this, he might not have been granted that most important patent number, 174,465, for his invention of the telephone.

A newspaper article announces the extension of the transcontinental phone line to include Boston. ▶

BOSTON CALLS SAN FRANCISCO

Direct Telephone Line Open Across the Continent

SPEECH CARRIED 3500 MILES

Bell Telephone Engineers Extend Long Distance Line to the Pacific Coast---Science and Inventive Genius Finally Overcome Great Obstacles

WHAT IT MEANS TO TELEPHONE FROM BOSTON TO SAN FRANCISCO.

Distance—3505 miles.

Twelve States Covered.

Miles of Copper Wire—14,020.

Weight of Wire—Over 3000 tons.

Poles on Line—Over 140,000.

Speed—One-fifteenth of second.

Crossing the continent—from Boston to San Francisco—in one-fifteenth of a second is an actual accomplishment. Direct conversation between the two cities so far apart was established for the first time, the other day, over the longest telephone line in the world—more than 3500 miles.

The successful consummation of this great work is an epoch in history—the acme of telephone attainment. It is an achievement made possible only by the scientific study and persistent effort of the engineers of the great Bell system.

Professor Bell's First Telephone

Think for a moment what the opening of the Boston-San Francisco direct line means. It has made Massachusetts and California neighbors. It will carry the business message from the Atlantic to the Pacific quicker than a man can write a letter and it gives him an answer at once. It has annihilated distance. Its commercial value is priceless.

Boston Men Built the Line

Across twelve states! Do you realize what that means? Have you ever traveled to the far west? On the fastest trains, it takes five days and five nights—120 hours—to go from Boston to San Francisco. And yet it will only be a little while before the business man can sit comfortably in his office and travel instantly by telephone between the two cities over tons of copper wire.

The opening of this line has a peculiar significance to the people of Boston and New England, for it was in Boston that Professor Alexander Graham Bell invented the telephone in 1876, less than forty years ago. A little later the longest toll line in the world stretched from Boston to Lowell and the service was poor and intermittent. How marvellous has been the progress.

And the men who were associated with Bell in those telephone pioneer

Telephoning over such a great distance would have been absolutely impossible without another wonderful invention—the repeating, or loading coils. Without any technical description, it is sufficient to say that these loading coils are placed at various points along the line and give the electrical waves additional force and power.

The line from Boston to San Francisco runs direct to Buffalo, 455 miles; thence to Chicago, 605 miles, to Omaha 500 miles, to Denver 585 miles, to Salt Lake City 580 miles and to San Francisco 770 miles, a total of 3505 miles.

A spur line runs from Chicago to Pittsburg, 345 miles, and thence to New York, 390 miles. Another spur connects Buffalo and New York, 390 miles.

On the same day the line between Boston and San Francisco was opened telephone conversation was established between New York and San Francisco. Professor Bell talked from the New York end and his early associate, Thomas A. Watson, from San Francisco.

An interesting fact in connection with the opening of this line is that Professor Bell used at the New York end an exact reproduction of his first crude instrument. At first it could be used only a few feet. That that instrument could be used in talking between New York and San Francisco is due to the skill and inventions of those engineers who followed Bell after his retirement from the telephone business, in the perfection of the telephone and of switchboards, cables and the hundreds of other accessors to successful telephone transmission.

Looking Backward to the Beginning

On the evening of Oct. 9, 1876, the first long conversation over the telephone was made by Bell and Watson. They talked for three hours over a telegraph line between Boston and Cambridge. It was the wonder of the day. In May, 1877, a Charlestown man leased two telephones—the first money ever paid for telephone service. The same month the first tiny and crude telephone exchange was born with five telephones connected.

Inventor of the Telephone and the Man who Developed the Business.

ROUTE OF TRANSCONTINENTAL TELEPHONE LINES BOSTON TO SAN FRANCISCO, 3505 MILES

Bell's Earliest Associate and the World's Greatest Telephone Expert.

ALEXANDER GRAHAM BELL
THOMAS A. WATSON

THEODORE N. VAIL
JOHN J. CARTY

Four Telephone Pioneers Who Have Made It Possible to Talk From Boston to San Francisco, Over 3500 Miles, and to Whom the Opening of the Line Means More Than to Any Other Men in the World

As an event, it is on a parity with the opening of the Panama canal. It is another connecting link that physically binds the far east and the far west of America into one complete union.

days, and developed his great idea until one in every eight persons in the United States is connected by telephone, are Boston men. Many of them are living today.

By August there were 778 telephones in use—all in Boston—and four men had an absolute monopoly of the telephone business.

TIMELINE
Alexander Graham Bell's Life

1847
Aleck is born in Scotland.

1867
Younger brother Edward dies of tuberculosis.

1870
Older brother Melville dies of tuberculosis. Aleck and family move to Canada.

1871
Aleck moves to Boston, Massachusetts, to teach deaf pupils.

1872
Aleck begins experimenting with the harmonic telegraph.

1874
Aleck has the idea for a telephone. Tom Watson becomes his assistant.

1875
Gardiner Hubbard and Thomas Sanders sponsor Aleck's inventions.

1876
Aleck granted patent for telephone.

1800

1877
Aleck, Tom, and their sponsors form Bell Telephone Company.

1877–78
Aleck marries Mabel Hubbard. They demonstrate the telephone for Queen Victoria of England.

1880
Aleck wins the Volta Prize and sets up Volta Laboratory to encourage invention.

1907
Aleck and Mabel form Aerial Experiment Association (AEA) to experiment with flight.

1909
AEA makes first Canadian flight of a machine that is heavier than air.

1919
Hydrofoil invented by Aleck breaks world speed record on water.

1922
Aleck dies in Canada.

1900

TELEPHONES
THROUGH THE YEARS

See how telephones have changed over time. What would Alexander Graham Bell and Thomas Watson have thought of modern phones?

Earpiece

Bell signals an incoming call.

1879 ▶
This wall-hung telephone was invented by Thomas Edison. The user had to wind the crank.

Crank

Mouthpiece

◀1905
Picking up the earpiece of the candlestick model connected the caller to an operator.

1920s ▲
A handset phone with both the earpiece and mouthpiece became standard.

1930s ▲
A dial on the phone enabled the user to make a direct call without an operator.

1970s ▲
Push-button dialling used new technology called Touch-Tone.

1990s ▲
An electronic memory stored frequently used phone numbers.

NOW ►
Mobile phones use radio-wave signals so the user can make or receive calls from almost anywhere.

119

Telephone
Trivia

The word telephone
comes
from
ancient Greek.
tele = far away.
phone = sound.
tele + *phone* = far away sound.

Bell installed the first
telephone line
from the
shop of
Charles Williams, Jr,
at 109 Court Street to
Williams' home a few miles away.

The first words heard over
the telephone were,
"Mr. Watson -
come here -
I want to see you!"
Legend has it that
Aleck yelled this into the
transmitter after he had spilled
acid on his trousers, but the description
of the event in Bell's papers does
not support this story.

One of the first people to have
a telephone in his
home was
American
author Mark Twain,
whose books include
The Adventures of Tom Sawyer,
The Adventures of Huckleberry Finn,
and *The Prince and the Pauper.*

The first telephone in
the White House
was
installed
by President
Rutherford B. Hayes
in 1879. His made his first
call to Alexander Graham Bell.

In 1876, William Orton of Western
Union told Aleck: "Mr Bell,
after careful
consideration
of your invention,
while it is an
interesting novelty, we have
come to the conclusion that it has no
commercial possibilities.... What use could
this company make of an electrical toy?"

TELEPHONE QUIZ

See if you can find the answers to these questions about what you have read.

1. Where was Alexander Graham Bell born?

2. Aleck believed that vibrations, or sound waves, were key to both hearing and what other action?

3. Sound waves vibrate which part of the ear canal?

4. Aleck moved from Canada to which city in the United States of America?

5. What kind of students did Aleck teach?

6. Who was the young electrician who became Aleck's assistant?

7. Who were Aleck's sponsors?

8. What document protects an invention so other people cannot make, sell or use it without permission?

9. What was the name of the biggest telegraph company in the world?

10. Aleck's multiple telegraph used sound tones to send many signals at once. What did he call it?

11. Who was Aleck's wife?

12. What was the 'first real sound to be transmitted electrically', which Aleck heard through the telephone receiver on 2nd June, 1875?

13. What was Lewis Latimer's job?

14. Who submitted his patent application for the telephone only two hours after Aleck?

15. In which year did Aleck receive the patent for the telephone?

Answers on page 125.

GLOSSARY

Caveat
Official notice or warning.

Electromagnet
Magnet wrapped in a coil of wire that has an electric current passing through it.

Elocution
Study of how to speak clearly and expressively.

Frequency
Rate per second of a vibration, making a sound wave or electronic wave.

Harmonic
Series of frequencies that make up a signal or sound pattern.

Molecules
Unit of a substance, made up of two or more tiny particles called atoms.

Patent
Government license giving right of ownership for an invention.

Quadruplex
Telegraph system where two messages can be sent in each direction and at the same time over one wire.

Resistance
Force that tries to stop an electric current flow through an electrical circuit.

Sponsor
Person providing money for a project or activity that another person is doing.

Telegraph
System for sending a message along a long-distance wire, using electrical signals.

Transatlantic
Crossing the Atlantic Ocean.

Transmitter
Device for producing and sending electrical signals.

Vibrate
Move rapidly to and fro.

INDEX

Answers To Telephone Quiz

1. Edinburgh, Scotland; **2.** Speaking; **3.** Eardrum; **4.** Boston; **5.** Deaf people; **6.** Tom Watson; **7.** Thomas Sanders and Gardiner Hubbard; **8.** Patent; **9.** Western Union; **10.** Harmonic telegraph; **11.** Mabel Hubbard; **12.** The twanging of the reed; **13.** Professional draughtsman; **14.** Elisha Gray; **15.** 1876.

Guide for Parents

DK Reads is a three-level interactive reading adventure series for children, developing the habit of reading widely for both pleasure and information. These chapter books have an exciting main narrative interspersed with a range of reading genres to suit your child's reading ability, as required by the National Curriculum. Each book is designed to develop your child's reading skills, fluency, grammar awareness, and comprehension in order to build confidence and engagement when reading.

Ready for a *Reading Alone* book

YOUR CHILD SHOULD

- be able to read independently and silently for extended periods of time.
- read aloud flexibly and fluently, in expressive phrases with the listener in mind.
- respond to what they are reading with an enquiring mind.

A VALUABLE AND SHARED READING EXPERIENCE

Supporting children when they are reading proficiently can encourage them to value reading and to view reading as an interesting, purposeful and enjoyable pastime. So here are a few tips on how to use this book with your child.

TIP 1 Reading aloud as a learning opportunity:

- if your child has already read some of the book, ask him/her to explain the earlier part briefly.
- encourage your child to read slightly slower than his/her normal silent reading speed so that the words are clear and the listener has time to absorb the information, too.

Reading aloud provides your child with practice in expressive reading and performing to a listener, as well as a chance to share his/her responses to the storyline and the information.

TIP 2 Praise, share and chat:

- encourage your child to recall specific details after each chapter.
- provide opportunities for your child to pick out interesting words and discuss what they mean.
- discuss how the author captures the reader's interest, or how effective the non-fiction layouts are.
- ask the questions provided on some pages and in the quiz. These help to develop comprehension skills and awareness of the language used.
- ask if there's anything that your child would like to discover more about.

Further information can be researched in the index of other non-fiction books or on the Internet.

A FEW ADDITIONAL TIPS

- Continue to read to your child regularly to demonstrate fluency, phrasing and expression; to find out or check information; and for sharing enjoyment.
- Encourage your child to read a range of different genres, such as newspapers, poems, review articles and instructions.
- Provide opportunities for your child to read to a variety of eager listeners, such as a sibling or a grandparent.

Have you read these other great books from DK?

Encounter the rare animals in the mountain forests of Cambodia.

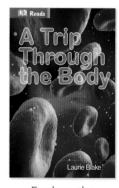

Explore the amazing systems at work inside the human body.

Step back nearly 20,000 years to the days of early cave dwellers.

Lift the bonnet on the inner workings of cars and bikes. Which team will win the race?

Be a rock detective! Unravel the clues to identify and classify the rocks.

Discover the fascinating world of creepy-crawlies in the Amazon rainforest.